"The best book available for children with OCD"

Charles Mansueto, Ph.D., Scientific Advisory Board, Obsessive-Compulsive Foundation

Up and Down the Worry Hill

A Children's Book about
Obsessive-Compulsive Disorder and its Treatment

By Aureen Pinto Wagner, Ph.D. Illustrations by Paul A. Jutton

A Lighthouse Press Book

Publisher's Cataloging-in-Publication

Wagner, Aureen Pinto.
    Up and down the worry hill : a children's book about obsessive-compulsive disorder and its treatment / by Aureen Pinto Wagner ; illustrations by Paul A. Jutton. -- 2nd ed
    p. cm.
    SUMMARY: Examination of compulsive behavior emphasizes that many people have this disorder and discusses its causes, effects, and treatment options.
    Audience: Ages 4-14.
    LCCN 2004092498
    ISBN-10: 0-9677347-6-2
    ISBN-13: 978-0-9677347-6-7

    1. Obsessive-compulsive disorder in children-- Juvenile literature. 2. Obsessive-compulsive disorder. I. Jutton, Paul A., ill. II. Title.

RJ506.O25W34 2004   618.92'85227
                           QBI33-2026

First edition April 2000
Second edition May 2004

Library of Congress Control Number: 2004092498

Published by Lighthouse Press, Inc.

Toll free USA and Canada: 1-888-749-8768

www.Lighthouse-Press.com

ISBN-13: 978-0-9677347-6-7

ISBN-10: 0-9677347-6-2

WORRY HILL® Registered in the U.S. Patent and Trademark office.

Sixth Printing

Printed in the United States of America

CPSIA Section 103
Tracking Label for
Lead-free Compliance
Printer: Josten's Printing & Publishing
29625 Rd. 84
PO Box 991
Visalia, CA 93291
Run No: E277990
Date: March, 2010

to all the courageous children who have taught me about

the struggles and victories of being a child with OCD.

With thanks to my husband, Scott, who first inspired me to write this book,

and with whose continued support this book was made possible,

to our children Catherine and Ethan, and to my parents and family

for their love and confidence in me through the years.

Preface for Parents and Professionals

When children experience obsessions and compulsions, they are often scared, confused, ashamed and defensive, as they cannot explain their uncontrollable worries and senseless rituals. **Up and Down the Worry Hill** is written to dispel the fears and uncertainties of these children. Children need to know that they are not alone and that neither they nor their parents are to blame. They need to know that help is available and that they can have a significant impact on their own treatment and recovery.

In the course of my experience in treating Obsessive-Compulsive Disorder (OCD), I developed a child-friendly approach to convey these messages to youngsters. Many parents asked me to write a book, so that other families could benefit from the same understanding of this beguiling illness. So was born **Up and Down the Worry Hill**.

Up and Down the Worry Hill describes OCD from a child's perspective. It provides accurate information about OCD and offers parents, educators and clinicians the chance to engage in an open discussion of a baffling illness. It attempts to give children with OCD a sense of control and hope. Hope and optimism are critical in building the readiness and persistence that it takes to gain mastery over OCD.

Most importantly, **Up and Down the Worry Hill** helps children prepare to engage in treatment. It describes **Cognitive-Behavioral Therapy** (CBT), a highly effective treatment for OCD, in a manner that children can comprehend. This book uses real-life metaphors to describe the concepts of CBT. Metaphors simplify difficult and abstract concepts by comparing them to situations that children can easily understand. The metaphor of the Worry Hill evolved over the years in my work with children with OCD. Children and adults have responded very favorably to it.

The first edition of **Up and Down the Worry Hill**, published in 2000, received an overwhelming response. This second edition builds on the first, with more comprehensive coverage of the concepts, process and steps involved in CBT and recovery.

To make the best use of this book, read and discuss this story several times with your child. Repeated readings will help your child absorb and integrate the many complexities of OCD and CBT gradually. Young children may benefit from having segments of the book read to them at different times. Reading this book to siblings and classmates of children with OCD may help them be more empathic and supportive.

This book has two companion books that capitalize on the synergy of the parent-child-therapist team in conquering OCD. **What to do when your Child has Obsessive-Compulsive Disorder: Strategies and Solutions** offers parents and educators step-by-step practical guidance in helping children triumph over OCD. **Treatment of OCD in Children and Adolescents: Professional's Kit** provides therapists with in-depth description of the Four-Phase Worry Hill treatment approach and specific protocols for effectively treating various forms of OCD. Information on these companion books is available at the back of this book.

May your ride **Up and Down the Worry Hill** be victorious!

Aureen P. Wagner, Ph.D.

Casey woke up and rubbed his eyes. It was a bright and sunny day.

He was happy and wanted to ride the new bicycle his parents gave him. He had been practicing everyday and could ride it quite well.

Casey's dad had promised that he would teach Casey how to ride up the Big Hill at the end of the street and then coast down it. Casey had been waiting to do that for a long time. Today was the day...

Casey sat up in bed. He picked up Teddy and touched him four times.
Then he got out of bed carefully, with one foot first, then the other.

He patted his pillow four times and tucked his sheets all around it.

Casey smiled. "It feels just right. Now I'll have a perfect day."

"Mom, I'm up! I really want to ride my new bike."

"Come on down, Casey," replied his mother. "Dad and Jenny are up too.
It's time for breakfast, and then off to school you go. You can ride your bike when you
get home from school in the afternoon."

Casey started to get dressed for school. He put on his "special" pants. They felt right. Then he picked out the socks that felt good on his toes. He had many other pairs of socks but the bumps on the seams bothered his feet.

Casey was just leaving his room when he wondered if he'd said a bad word. He shook his head as he tried to shake the thought out.

He counted the stairs as he went down. "That wasn't right," he said.
He came back up and counted them again.
And again.

"I wish I could get it right the first time," Casey sighed.

"Look, Casey, I made muffins for you,"
said his mother, giving him a hug.
"Oh, goody! My favorite kind," grinned
Casey. "But my hands feel dirty.
I have to wash them."

Casey scrubbed his hands
well and rinsed them.
Then he looked
at them carefully.
"They still feel yucky.
What if they still have
germs on them?"
He washed his hands again.

Casey's mother came in. "Are you
done washing, dear?" Casey was getting
frustrated. "My hands feel germy.
I have to wash them again."

Casey's mother looked at his hands.
"They're very clean. Turn off the
faucet. You'll be late for school,"
she said.
Casey looked at his mother. "I can't! Please, can you turn it off for me?"
Casey's mother turned off the faucet and helped him out of the bathroom.

Casey sat down for breakfast after giving his dad a hug.

His sister Jenny ate her muffins fast.
His parents sipped their coffee and talked
about riding in the park on their new bicycles.

But Casey wasn't listening. He was busy cutting his muffin up into small pieces, all the
same size. He ate one piece on one side of his mouth, then took one sip of milk, and ate
the next piece on the other side of his mouth.

Then he repeated it all over again.

Casey's mother looked at the clock. "Hurry, Casey, it's almost time for the bus! Just take a few bites all at once and you'll be done before you know it."

Casey looked at his plate. He had seven bites left and he had to finish them in the right order.

"I can't eat any faster. I have to do it exactly it this way," he whispered to himself.

Jenny laughed at him. "C'mon Casey-man, what's the matter? Can't you hurry, slow-poke?" I saw you this morning, touching and counting things in your room. You're weird, Casey!"

Casey was sad. He finished his breakfast just in time for the school bus. Then he had to check his book bag to make sure he hadn't forgotten his homework. He counted his books, pencils and erasers.

Jenny started talking just then, and Casey thought he made a mistake. He checked and counted again, just to be sure.

"Mom, you saw me do my homework, right? Did I put it in my bag?" Casey was frantic as he rushed out the door.

"Be safe, be well,
don't slip, don't fall,
goodbye, goodluck…"
Casey muttered his
goodluck charm
under his breath.

At school, the teacher, Mrs. Kelly, talked about the special project for the day.
"We're going to learn about the sun, moon and the planets today.
Then you can draw and paint them!"

Casey was excited. He knew lots of things about the planets and he couldn't wait to say them. Then suddenly, he felt scared. He thought about drawing and painting the planets. What if the paint got on his hands and he couldn't wash it off? Would it make him sick?

He asked Mrs. Kelly if he would get sick. "No, Casey, you'll be fine," she replied. "Are you sure, Mrs. Kelly? I won't vomit?" "You know that already, Casey. It's time to start your project." But Casey couldn't stop thinking about it.

Casey began to draw the planets. He wanted his drawing to be perfect. The circles didn't come out right, so he erased them and drew them again. It still wasn't perfect. Casey erased it again. The paper tore.

Casey was getting tired. The other kids had finished their drawings and were already painting.

Everyone else was having fun. Why couldn't he be like them? Casey felt ashamed and hid his drawing.

Alex and Laura were sitting next to Casey. Alex said, "Hey, how come you're always the last one to finish, Casey? Laura leaned over and said, "Let me see your drawing! Look, the paper's torn. Why do you erase it so much?"

Casey looked away. He didn't know what to say. He wished he could hide somewhere or disappear. He couldn't wait to get home.

Mrs. Kelly came over to Casey's desk and asked if he needed help. Casey tried to hide his face. "No thanks, I'm fine," he muttered.

Finally, it was time for Casey to go home. He was exhausted. The only thing he looked forward to was riding his bicycle with his dad.

At last, Casey's dad was home from work. It was time to ride up the Big Hill! Casey and his father put on their helmets and off they went.

Dad said, "Remember, Casey, it's hard work going up a hill. You have to keep going a little at a time. I'm right here with you if you need help."

"I really want to do it, Dad! I know I can!"

As they went up the hill, Casey began huffing and puffing. He kept saying, "I can do it, little by little."

And then...

Before he knew it, he was at the top! He was hot and tired, but beaming. "I did it, Daddy, I did it," he yelled out.

Then came the best part. It was time to coast down the hill. "Now, we can enjoy the ride down the hill," Casey's dad called out.

"Wheeee, here I come!" said Casey as he and his dad coasted down Big Hill. The breeze blew in his face and his hair. He was thrilled as he rode all the way down.

Casey was laughing. He hadn't had so much fun in a long time.

Casey and his father rested at the bottom of Big Hill.
"You're a great kid, Casey," smiled his father, patting him on the back.

"But Dad, the kids at school think I'm silly or crazy. I can't do anything right."

"No one gets everything right the first time, Casey.
You're not crazy, and Mom and I love you the same, no matter what."

That night, Casey's mother came to say goodnight. She sat at his bedside. "You look tired and sad, Casey. Is everything okay? I saw you checking under your bed. Mrs. Kelly said you were trying very hard to get your drawing right at school."

Casey's eyes filled with tears. "Mom, I'm scared that if I don't do things perfectly, something bad will happen. Why do I have to do that? How come Jenny doesn't need to do that?"

Casey's mother kissed him on the forehead. "Nobody's perfect, Casey. Each kid is different in his or her own way," she replied. "But that doesn't mean that you are not good or smart. Dad and I found a doctor we can talk to about your worries. We'll go see Dr. Greene tomorrow. She's a child psychologist and she'll know how to help us."

Casey felt better after that. He sighed with relief and went to sleep.

Casey was nervous about talking to Dr. Greene, but she was kind. She listened as Casey and his parents told her about his worries and the things he had to repeat.

"Casey, do you like doing things over again till you get them right?" asked Dr. Greene. "No, I wish I could stop! I'd like to play and have fun like the other kids."

"What happens if you try to stop, Casey?" asked Dr. Greene. "I feel kind of scared and weird. Sometimes, I worry about bad luck, and I can't stop thinking about it. Sometimes I don't know why, but I just have to do it a certain way."

"Is there something wrong with me, Dr. Greene? Am I the only one who has to do things this way?"

"No, Casey, all of us worry and we like to do things a certain way. But, sometimes, people can't stop worrying because they have **Obsessive-Compulsive Disorder**. It's called OCD for short. Let me tell you a little bit about OCD.

You see, Casey, when you have OCD, your brain sends you a lot of worry messages that get stuck in your mind even when there's no reason to be worried.

It's like it would be if you rang the doorbell and the button got stuck. The doorbell would keep ringing and ringing and wouldn't stop. OCD is like a "worry bell" in your brain that gets stuck and doesn't stop.

The worry thoughts that OCD sends you are called **obsessions**. The things you do over and over again to make the worries go away are called **compulsions** or **rituals**."

Casey was surprised to hear that he had OCD and that it happened in his brain. "So it's not just my fault that I do weird things, is it Dr. Greene?" he asked.

"Not at all! Having OCD is not your fault. It's not your parents' fault either. It's like having allergies or asthma—it happens to you because you're more sensitive to it. There may be other people in your family who also have OCD because they are sensitive to it.

OCD isn't something you do on purpose to get attention or because you're lazy. Sometimes, your parents, teachers and friends may think that you are just being stubborn or annoying. It's hard for them to understand that you don't want to do it, but you don't know how to stop."

Casey's parents nodded their heads. Casey smiled. Dr. Greene really did understand!

"Casey, do you know that there are many other kids and adults who have OCD? You're not the only one!

Everyone's OCD can be a little different—people can have obsessions about someone getting hurt or bad luck happening. Sometimes, they may even have thoughts that they've said or done something really bad when they actually haven't. Rituals can also be of many types, like checking things, counting, cleaning or saying sorry all the time."

Casey thought about what Dr. Greene was saying. He knew he was not alone. He knew he wasn't bad or crazy. But would he get better? Could he be like the other kids?

"Will I always have to do things over and over, Dr. Greene?"

Dr. Greene smiled. "Well, guess what? I have some good news for you! There are some ways to fix the "worry bell" in your brain when it gets stuck. One way is called **Cognitive-Behavioral Therapy** or CBT for short.

With CBT, you will understand that you're in charge, not OCD. You can choose what you want to think and do. You will learn how to face your OCD worries and realize that they don't come true. Then you will learn how to do the opposite of what OCD tells you to do. You'll be surprised to find that nothing bad will happen when you stop doing the things OCD tells you to do.

It's a lot like riding a bicycle. Do you ride a bicycle, Casey?"

"Yes, I rode up a big hill yesterday and then I came coasting down. It was hard work to get up the hill, but lots of fun coming down," said Casey with sparkling eyes.

27

"Well, Casey, in the beginning, facing your fears and stopping your rituals feels like riding up a big Worry Hill because it's hard work. You huff and you puff up the hill. If you keep going and don't give up, you get to the top of the Worry Hill. Once you get to the top, you find out that your fears don't come true! Then, it's easy to ride down the hill. You can only coast down the hill if you first get to the top.

Getting to the top of the Worry Hill takes patience and hard work. The more you practice, the easier it gets.

I will teach you some exercises called **exposure** and **ritual prevention** that will help you face your fears without doing the rituals. You will learn to face your fears one step at a time. What's the best way to prepare for riding up a big hill, Casey?"

"Try some smaller hills first?" Casey ventured.

"Yes, exactly! You start with the little hills and gradually work your way up to the big ones. You get stronger with each hill, and the big hill won't seem so big anymore. In the same way, you will learn to face your fears gradually, not all at once.

I will **guide** you, you will **ride** up and down the Worry Hill, and your parents will **rally** for you and cheer you on. We will all work together as a team to help you ride as well as you can."

"Another way to make OCD better is to take medicine. The medicine may help the worry bell in your brain work properly again. It takes a few weeks to make the OCD better, and sometimes, it takes a while to find the right medicine.

Not everyone with OCD needs medicine. Some kids need both medicine and CBT to get better. Medicine can sometimes make it easier to learn CBT, just like training wheels make it easier to learn how to ride a bicycle. But, to be in charge, you still have to learn to ride up and down the Worry Hill."

Casey sat back in his chair. Suddenly, he didn't feel crazy, scared or confused any more. "Wow, I don't have to believe or do what OCD tells me anymore..." He liked that idea a lot. "Yes, Dr. Greene!" he exclaimed. "I want to learn the CBT exercises to make the OCD go away. I want to be in charge!"

Casey's parents were relieved. "We'll do everything to help you learn how to beat OCD," said his father.

Casey began to see Dr. Greene every week. He learned the exposure and ritual prevention exercises.

Little by little, Casey learned how to do the opposite of what OCD wanted him to do. He walked down the stairs without counting them, washed his hands only once before eating, took big bites of his muffin and went to the bus stop without checking his book bag.

Dr. Greene was right! At first, he felt worried and scared when he didn't do the rituals, but nothing bad happened! Pretty soon, the scared feeling just went away!

Casey practiced the new things he learned everyday. The more he practiced, the less worried he felt, and the easier it became. The "worry bell" didn't seem to get stuck so much anymore.

Dr. Greene also taught Casey's parents new ways to help Casey ride up and down the Worry Hill and to be patient and understanding while he learned.

"I'm in charge now, Dr. Greene," Casey burst out with pride. "You're right, Casey," replied Dr. Greene. "But remember, no matter how well you ride or how much you practice, there will be times when you wobble or fall off the bicycle. So what would you do if you fell off your bicycle?" "I'd get up and see if I need a bandaid. Or maybe I'd have to go to the doctor if I got hurt bad." "And after you've taken care of it, would you ride your bicycle again?" "Oh, yes, I'd get on my bicycle as soon as I could."

Dr. Greene nodded. "Casey, sometimes you may have an OCD "slip" or "fall" no matter how well you ride. It may happen when you are tired or not feeling well. It's no different than falling off a bicycle. You pick yourself up, fix the problem, and ride that Worry Hill again."

Casey started feeling a lot better. After a few weeks, he noticed that he didn't worry as much or feel sad anymore. He didn't have to touch things four times any more. He could eat his muffins just as fast as Jenny did! His clothes didn't feel so funny now. His hands didn't feel so "germy" anymore. He even forgot to check his book bag before he ran off to school!

Most of all, he found out that he didn't have to be perfect! He was having fun like the other kids.

Then one day, Casey
rode his bicycle up the Big
Hill all by himself! He wasn't huffing
and puffing as much anymore. He got to
the top quickly and looked around. He was so
proud of himself. Then it was time for his
favorite part--coasting down the Big Hill. As he
breezed past the bushes and trees, he whistled a tune
and thought to himself, "I learned how to ride up the hill
and I learned how to face my OCD. I want to tell all the
kids with OCD who feel alone, ashamed and sad, Don't give up! You
too can learn how to beat OCD by riding up and down the Worry Hill."

Casey sang softly to himself, "Up the hill, down the hill, on my new
bicycle........."

ADDITIONAL RESOURCES

Anxiety Disorders Association of America (ADAA)
8730 Georgia Avenue, Suite 600 Silver Spring, MD 20910
240 485-1001   www.adaa.org

Association for Behavioral and Cognitive Therapies (ABCT)
305 Seventh Avenue, 16th Floor   New York, NY 10001-6008
212 647-1890   www.abct.org

Lighthouse Press, Inc.
www.lighthouse-press.com

Obsessive-Compulsive Foundation
P.O. Box 961029 Boston, MA 02196
www.ocfoundation.org

Obsessive Compulsive Information Center (OCIC)
7617 Mineral Point Road Suite 300   Madison, WI 53717
608 827-2470   www.miminc.org

Tourette Syndrome Association
42-40 Bell Boulevard   New York, NY 11361
718 224-2999   www.tsa-usa.org

"The best book available for Children with OCD"

- Charles Mansueto, Ph.D., Scientific Advisory Board, Obsessive-Compulsive Foundation

Now on Audio CD

Listen as Aureen Wagner, Ph.D. award winning author and internationally recognized expert in the treatment of childhood OCD reads:

Up and Down the Worry Hill: A Children's Book about Obsessive-Compulsive Disorder and its Treatment.

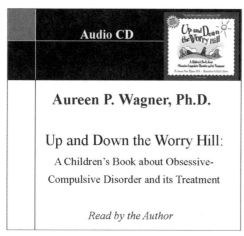

Audio CD

Aureen P. Wagner, Ph.D.

Up and Down the Worry Hill:

A Children's Book about Obsessive-Compulsive Disorder and its Treatment

Read by the Author

Item Number 4789
$19.95

Appropriate for children with OCD,

siblings and classmates

- Casey's Worries and Habits
- Casey Gets Help
- Note for Parents/Professionals

- Audio CD
- Running time approximately 27 minutes

Three easy ways to order: Quick Order Form at the back of this book
or call 1-888-749-8768 (Toll Free, US and Canada)
or online at www.Lighthouse-Press.com (secure site)

What to do when your Child has Obsessive Compulsive Disorder: Strategies and Solutions

The Companion Guide to: <u>Up and Down the Worry Hill</u>
For parents, adolescents and families

"<u>Must reading</u> for parents of children with OCD. Clearly the work of a skilled and compassionate clinician. Just as important, it makes interesting reading."

Judith Rapoport, M.D., Chief, Child Psychiatry Branch, National Institute of Mental Health

Using the compelling Worry Hill approach, Dr. Wagner provides families with the blueprint to triumph over OCD.

- Step-by-step practical guidance
- Unlocks the power of the parent-child team to conquer OCD
- Practical, clear and easy-to-understand steps
- The latest scientifically proven advances in treatment

What the experts say:

"Every parent who has a child with OCD should read this book.
I will recommend it from now on."

Michael Jenike, M.D., Harvard Medical School

"A "must read," essential book...just the right balance of medical background and practical advice...filled with pearls of wisdom..."

Roger Kurlan, M.D., Medical Advisory Board, Tourette Syndrome Association

"A truly remarkable guide for parents, clinicians and school personnel.
Expertly written and organized..."

John Piacentini, Ph.D., Director, UCLA Child OCD, Anxiety and Tic Disorders Program

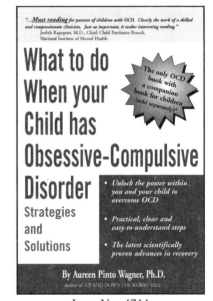

Item No. 4711
$19.95

Three easy ways to order: Quick Order Form at the back of this book
or call 1-888-749-8768 (Toll Free, US and Canada)
or online at www.Lighthouse-Press.com (secure site)

Putting the Groundbreaking
Worry Hill Treatment Approach for OCD
into action!

Treatment of OCD in Children and Adolescents: Professional's Kit

Item Number 9226 $139.95
For clinicians

This newly revised and expanded popular resource for professionals includes second editions of both the Therapy Manual and Teaching Tools. Dr. Wagner shares her internationally acclaimed Worry Hill protocol for OCD, along with clinical pearls from her may years of experience. She provides expert guidance on special topics including:

- Developing treatment readiness
- Collaborating with parents
- Working with reluctant children
- Overcoming treatment challenges

The Professional's Kit includes:

1. Cognitive-Behavorial Therapy Manual (Expanded Second Edition)

2. Complete set of thirty 8.5" x 11" Teaching Tools (Comb bound, Second Edition)

3. Over 35 ready-to-print-and-use forms on CD (*PC only*)

4. Worry Hill Memory Cards and Feeling Thermometers for use in working with children and families

Benefits:

- User-friendly and appealing
- Step-by-step protocols
- Easy application and record-keeping
- Clear and self-explanatory
- Detailed case examples

"This manual is the **best available resource for clinicians**...clear, concise and accurate...with a rich supply of clinical insights and practical tips. I highly recommend it to all practitioners, from beginners to seasoned clinicians."

Charles Mansueto, Ph.D., Scientific Advisory Board, Obsessive Compulsive Foundation

"This is a **valuable** treatment manual for youngsters with OCD. **I recommend it with enthusiasm!**"

Judith Rapoport, M.D., Chief Child Psychiatry, National Institute of Mental Health

Worried No More:
Help and Hope for Anxious Children

For parents, school personnel and healthcare professionals

In this second edition of her landmark book, Dr. Wagner provides scientifically proven and time-tested strategies to help children overcome worry, school refusal, separation anxiety, excessive shyness, panic, disasters, phobias, obsessions and compulsions

Includes:

- How to tell normal anxiety from problem anxiety
- Different forms of anxiety in children and teenagers
- Red flags for anxiety
- Expressions of anxiety in school
- How to find the right professional help

- Effective treatments
- Dos and don'ts of parenting
- Step-by-step plans with examples
- Ready-to-use forms and tools
- An appealing approach to treatment

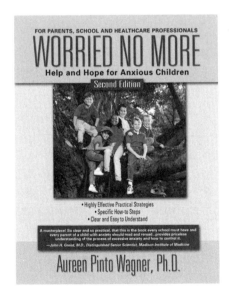

Item No. 4797
$24.95

Highly acclaimed by experts:

"A masterpiece...so clear and so practical, that this is the book every school must have and every parent of a child with anxiety should read and reread...provides priceless understanding of the process of excessive anxiety and how to control it."
  John H. Greist, M.D., Distinguished Senior Scientist, Madison Institute of Medicine

"A very helpful and practical book...immensely helpful...I highly recommend it!"
Michael Jenike, M.D., Harvard Medical School

"This excellent book could not be timelier considering the recent highly stressful events in our country. Scientific, yet highly readable, for professionals and non-professionals."
Sara S. Sparrow, Ph.D., Professor and Chief Psychologist, Yale University Child Study Center

For more information and reviews, visit www.Lighthouse-Press.com

Worried No More: Teaching Tools and Forms on CD

The companion kit for school professionals and therapists. This toolkit helps professionals put Worried No More into action with anxious children and their families. It includes 26 colorful Teaching Tools (easy-to-use, 8.5 x 11" flip cards), ready-to-use Microsoft® Powerpoint® slides (Viewer software included), ready-to-print-and-use Forms on CD (Adobe® Reader® software included) and Feeling Thermometers to convey key treatment concepts. .

Benefits:
- Powerful visual tools for teaching
- Appealing to children and families
- Increases motivation and compliance
- Improves communication and learning
- Convenient, easy-to-use
- Enhances record keeping

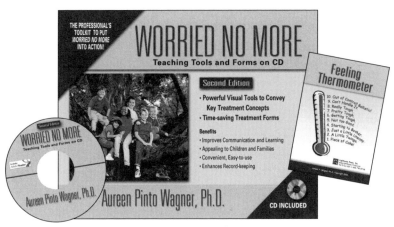

Item Number 4754 $59.95
Software for use with PC's only

Teaching Tools (sample)
- The Anxiety Triad
- The Noise at the Window
- Physical Signs of Worry
- The Vicious Cycle of Avoidance
- Lessons to be Learned
- Calm Thinking
- Exposure
- Habituation
- Anticipatory Anxiety
- Up and Down the Worry Hill
- The 3 P's of Parenting
- Appropriate Attending
- The Fearmometer
- Self-Reliance

Forms
·Corrective Learning Experiences
·Parent-Teacher Log
·Home Behavior Observations
·School Behavior Observations
·My Thoughts and Feelings
·The Feeling Thermometer
·My Fear Ladder
·Exposure Progress Record
·The Worry Hill Memory Card
·Facing My Fears

To order, see the Quick Order Form at the back of this book or contact Lighthouse Press at 1-888-749-8768 (Toll Free in the US) or visit our website at www.Lighthouse-Press.com

Anxiety and OCD at School:
Live Workshop for School Professionals

This workshop is ideal for a broad range of school staff, including:

- Mainstream and Special Education Teachers
- Teacher's Aides
- Counselors
- Social Workers
- Speech and Occupational Therapists
- Administrators
- School Psychologists

Item Number 4770 $49.95
For use with personal computers (PC)
with a CD-ROM drive.
Printable 21 page handout.

An audio and slide presentation recorded during one of Dr. Wagner's most popular workshops for School Professionals. Just like a real workshop, you'll listen to Dr. Wagner as you view the slides that accompany the presentation, and follow along with the handout. Packed with practical advice, you'll want to listen to this presentation repeatedly. This CD is ideal for staff development trainings or inservices. Dr. Wagner is a highly engaging and sought-after speaker whose workshops consistently receive outstanding reviews. You'll benefit from her many years of working with anxious children, her user-friendly conceptualizations and her practical Worry Hill innovations.

Comments from Recent Participants

"On a scale of 1 to 10, this **was a definite 10!** Most helpful were the practical strategies for anxiety."

"**Great, great speaker!** Best workshop I have attended in many years (in 28 years as a professional)."

Anxiety and OCD Workshops

Dr. Aureen Wagner offers a variety of workshops on anxiety and OCD for Parents, Schools and Healthcare Professionals.

Testimonials from recent workshops:

❏ "Thank you for the wonderful workshop you presented on anxiety... I was extremely pleased with the turnout and the response. Thank you for all your time and effort in tailoring your presentation to meet our needs."

❏ "This was an excellent workshop on OCD. Information was presented in a thorough, concrete manner to "grip" the attention of a diversely trained audience. I fully appreciated the inclusion of the discussion on adolescents, especially high school age students."

❏ "This is easily one of the best workshops I have ever attended. Thank you for the wonderful touch and the tremendous knowledge you bring to us."

❏ "Excellent presentation! Very helpful – warm, articulate and positive. Nice balance of lecture – large/small group."

Visit
www.Lighthouse-Press.com
for a complete description
of workshops

Feeling Thermometers - 20 Pieces

Item Number 9999   Price $9.95

....

Worry Hill Memory Cards – 20 Pieces

Item Number 9998   Price $19.95

....

Expert Clinician Consultation

Dr. Aureen Wagner provides consultation and supervision for healthcare professionals on assessment and treatment of anxiety disorders in children and adolescents. Consultation is tailored to suit your individual or group needs.

Topics:
- Assessment
- Differential diagnosis
- Treatment plans
- Exposure hierarchies
- Cognitive strategies
- Socratic technique
- Treatment reluctance
- Challenges in treatment

Telephone Sessions are scheduled via mutual convenience.
For more information on fees and scheduling, please send an email to:
Consultation@Lighthouse-Press.com or call (585) 594-4770

Special Offers

The Worry Hill Master Set For the Treatment of OCD

by Aureen Pinto Wagner, Ph.D.

Includes:
- Up and Down the Worry Hill
- What to do when your Child has OCD
- Treatment of OCD in Children and Adolescents:
  Professional's Kit

Order this set and save over $29.00!

Item No. 9993
$149.95

The Anxiety Treatment Master Set For the Treatment of Anxiety Problems

by Aureen Pinto Wagner, Ph.D.

Includes:
- Worried No More
- Worried No More: Teaching Tools and Forms on CD

Order this set and save over $10.00!

Item No. 9995
$74.90

The School Professionals Master Set

by Aureen Pinto Wagner, Ph.D.

Includes:
- Up and Down the Worry Hill
- Worried No More
- Worried No More:
  Teaching Tools and Forms on CD
- Anxiety and OCD at School:
  Live Workshop for School Professionals. PC CD-ROM

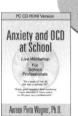

Order this set and save over $14.00!

Item No. 9997
$139.95

Lighthouse Press QUICK ORDER FORM

To place an order: **CALL** 1-888-749-8768 (Toll free, USA and Canada) or 1-585-594-0311
or **FAX** your Purchase Order to 1-585-594-4207
or **MAIL** your order to the address at the bottom of this form.

Item #	Name	Quantity	Unit Price*	Total Price
4762	Up and Down the Worry Hill		$19.95	

Prices subject to change

SUBTOTAL Price of items

Shipping (see chart below)

New York residents add 8% sales tax

TOTAL AMOUNT DUE

SHIPPING CHARGES: Within the U.S...............$5.00 for the first book, $3.00 for each additional book
Outside the U.S. ....$9.00 for the first book, $4.00 for each additional book

Payment Method:

❑ Check or Money Order made payable to Lighthouse Press, Inc. (Must be made payable through a U.S. bank and be in U.S. currency.)

❑ Visa   ❑ MasterCard   ❑ Discover   ❑ American Express

ACCOUNT NUMBER   EXPIRATION DATE

SIGNATURE (REQUIRED FOR CREDIT CARD ORDERS)

Ship to:

NAME

STREET ADDRSS

CITY   STATE   ZIP CODE

PHONE

Please Mail your completed order form with your check or money order to:
Lighthouse Press, Inc., 35 Ryans Run, Rochester, NY 14624

Free !

A printed color card of the
Feeling Thermometer
for easy use with your child

While supplies last

To customers in the USA only

To receive one, please send an email to
CustomerService@Lighthouse-Press.com with:
"Send Feeling Thermometer" in the subject line of the message
Please indicate the name of the book in which you saw this offer
and provide your name and mailing address in the body of the message

Or, send a postcard with the above information to:
Lighthouse Press, 35 Ryans Run, Rochester, NY 14624-1160

Lighthouse Press QUICK ORDER FORM

To place an order: CALL 1-888-749-8768 (Toll free, USA and Canada) or 1-585-594-0311

or **FAX** your Purchase Order to 1-585-594-4207

or **MAIL** your order to the address at the bottom of this form.

Item #	Name	Quantity	Unit Price*	Total Price
4762	Up and Down the Worry Hill		$19.95	

*Prices subject to change

SUBTOTAL Price of items ___

Shipping (see chart below) ___

New York residents add 8% sales tax ___

TOTAL AMOUNT DUE ___

SHIPPING CHARGES: Within the U.S..............$5.00 for the first book, $3.00 for each additional book

Outside the U.S. ....$9.00 for the first book, $4.00 for each additional book

Payment Method:

❏ Check or Money Order made payable to Lighthouse Press, Inc. (Must be made payable through a U.S. bank and be in U.S. currency.)

❏ Visa   ❏ MasterCard   ❏ Discover   ❏ American Express

ACCOUNT NUMBER _____ EXPIRATION DATE _____

SIGNATURE (REQUIRED FOR CREDIT CARD ORDERS) _____

Ship to:

NAME _____

STREET ADDRSS _____

CITY _____ STATE _____ ZIP CODE _____

PHONE _____

Please Mail your completed order form with your check or money order to:
Lighthouse Press, Inc., 35 Ryans Run, Rochester, NY 14624

DR. AUREEN PINTO WAGNER, is a member of the Scientific Advisory Board of the Obsessive Compulsive Foundation, Clinical Associate Professor of Neurology at the University of Rochester School of Medicine & Dentistry, and Director of The Anxiety Wellness Center in Rochester, NY. Dr. Wagner is a Clinical Child Psychologist whose unique Worry Hill® approach to making cognitive-behavioral therapy accessible to youngsters has gained her international recognition. She is the author of several highly acclaimed books. **Up and Down the Worry Hill**, her first book, was written for children with OCD and their families. It was followed by **What to do When Your Child has Obsessive-Compulsive Disorder: Strategies and Solutions**, written for parents and schools, and **Treatment of OCD in Children and Adolescents: Professional's Kit**, written for therapists. These three books comprise the only integrated set of resources for children with OCD, their patients and their therapists.

Dr. Wagner's fourth book, **Worried No More: Help and Hope for Anxious Children** provides parents, school and healthcare professionals with highly effective strategies to help children who experience separation anxiety, school refusal, excessive shyness, worries, phobias and panic.

Dr. Wagner received her education at St. Agnes College, the University of Iowa, Yale University Child Study Center and Brown University. Dr. Wagner is a highly engaging and sought-after speaker whose workshops for clinicians, school professionals and parents consistently receive outstanding reviews. Dr. Wagner lives in Rochester, NY with her family.

PAUL JUTTON is an artist and illustrator living in Washington DC. He studied graphic design at Rochester Institute of Technology.